Introduction

The *Cambridge Primary Science* series has been developed to match the Cambridge International Examinations Primary Science curriculum framework. It is a fun, flexible and easy to use course that gives both learners and teachers the support they need. In keeping with the aims of the curriculum itself, it encourages learners to be actively engaged with the content, and develop enquiry skills as well as subject knowledge.

This Activity Book for Stage 4 is designed to be used alongside the Learner's Book for the same stage, ISBN 978-1-107-67450-9.

In this book you will find a single-page exercise to accompany each topic presented in the Learner's Book, as well as a language review exercise at the end of each unit to practise the key vocabulary. The exercises are designed to be completed as pen-and-paper exercises, and learners can work on them individually or in pairs or small groups. You can set the exercises as in-class work or homework.

There are different styles of exercise throughout to maintain interest and to suit different purposes. The main aims of the exercises in this book are:

- to consolidate the subject knowledge presented in the Learner's Book
- to encourage learners to apply the knowledge in new situations, thus developing understanding
- to practise scientific language
- to develop scientific enquiry skills such as presenting and interpreting results from investigations.

The answers to the exercises in this Activity Book are available in the Teacher's Resource for Stage 4, ISBN 978-1-107-66151-6. This resource also contains extensive guidance on all the topics, ideas for classroom activities, and guidance notes on all the activities presented in the Learner's Book. You will also find a large collection of worksheets.

We hope you enjoy using this series.

With best wishes,
the Cambridge Primary Science team.

Contents

Useful words

arrange   to put things in a certain order or pattern

Lan will **arrange** the pasta shapes to make a skeleton.

apply   to do something with the help of knowledge you already have

Aruna will **apply** her knowledge of the particle theory to solve the problem.

bar chart   a chart that shows results using bars; the lengths of the bars show the sizes of the results

Yusef drew a **bar chart** to show the volume of water absorbed by different paper towels.

check   to make sure that you have done something correctly

You should always **check** your answers before you give your teacher your work.

choose   to select things from a group

Tabitha's aunt said she could **choose** which sweets she would like from all the sweets in the shop.

compare   to look at the similarities and differences between things

They will **compare** the weather in Mumbai and Qatar by looking at the monthly temperature and rainfall for each city.

complete	to finish something
	Ahmed will **complete** his work by the end of the lesson.
compress	to squash or squeeze
	Joseph will **compress** the air into the cylinder to allow him to swim underwater.
conclusion	a statement of what has been found out
	Bimla's **conclusion** was 'From the objects I have tested, only the paper clip is magnetic. The others are non-magnetic.'
demonstrate	to show somebody that you can do something
	Paula will **demonstrate** that she can sing in front of the class.
design	to plan something by sketches and written ideas
	Paulo liked making drawings to help him to **design** a new car.
identify	to recognise something from a group of things
	Long was able to **identify** an example of a frog from a group of animals.
instructions	information that tells you how to do something
	The book gave **instructions** on how to draw a graph.

investigate — to do a test or experiment to find something out

Meng was told to **investigate** which objects were magnetic.

label — to name the parts of something on a diagram

Juma will **label** six parts of a flower on the diagram in his science book.

list — to write or give examples of things, one after the other

I will **list** the things I need you to get at the shop.

measure — to find the mass, length or volume of something

Ranjit will **measure** how long his thigh bone is.

plan — to decide how to do an investigation

Ali wrote a **plan** to test different objects with a magnet.

practise — to do something several times so that you get better at doing it

Liam will **practise** the guitar every day until he can play the piece without a mistake.

predict — to think about what the result of an investigation might be

Aba was asked to **predict** which objects would be magnetic.

record   to write or draw to show what happened

Janis wrote the results in a table to **record** what happened.

research   to look for information by investigation or using books or the internet

Jamil used the internet to **research** magnetism.

results   the observations or measurements made in a test

Gopal's **results** showed that many objects were not magnetic.

suggest   to think of some examples to be considered

I will **suggest** three dishes that we can make for the birthday lunch.

table   a way of writing numbers or words in rows and columns

The **table** showed which objects were magnetic and which were non-magnetic.

Humans and animals

Exercise 1.1 Skeletons

In this exercise, you will match the skeletons with the animals they come from.
You will identify their bones and fill in a table.

1 Fill in the table.

Animal	Skeleton
bird	
rabbit	
frog	
crocodile	

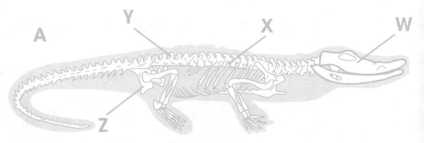

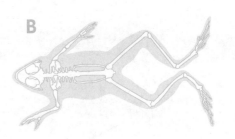

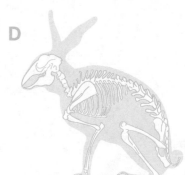

2 Write the names of the parts on skeleton A.

W is the _____ .

X is the _____ .

Y is the _____ .

Z is the _____ .

Exercise 1.2 The human skeleton

In this exercise, you will put bones in the right places to make
a human skeleton. You will label the bones.

1 Trace, or copy, the bones.

2 Cut them out and arrange them to make a skeleton.

3 Stick your skeleton onto a piece of paper.

4 Label the different bones on your skeleton using these words.

skull	ribs	thigh bone	upper arm bone
	finger bones	toe bones	hip bone	

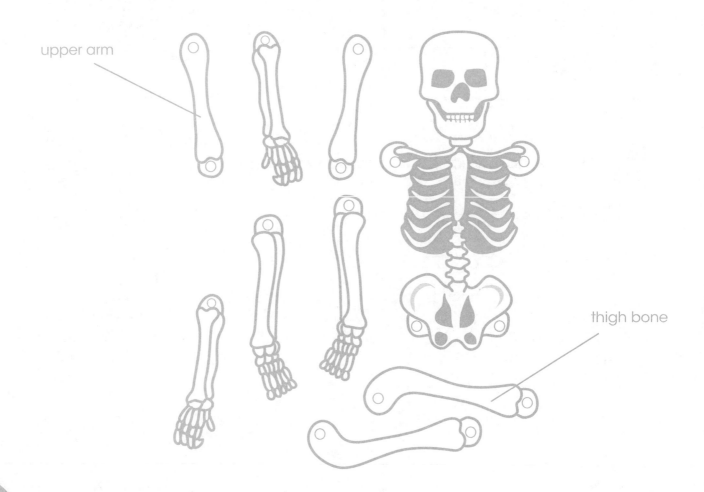

upper arm

thigh bone

Exercise 1.3   Why do we need a skeleton?

In this exercise, you will find information from a bar chart.

Nasreen measured the length of the upper arm bone of some people in her family. She drew this bar chart to show her results. Use the bar chart to answer the questions.

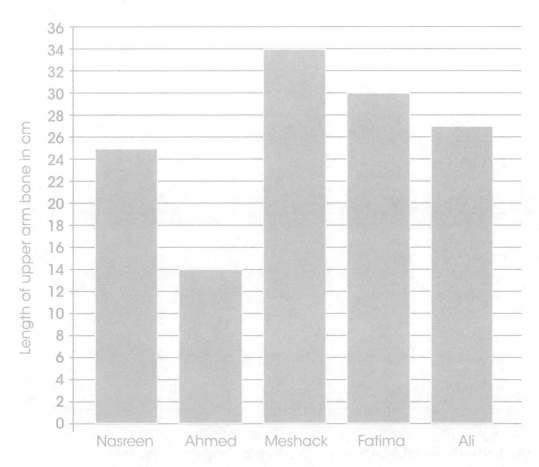

1 Who had the longest upper arm bone?

_____

2 How long is the shortest upper arm bone?

_____

3 Nasreen has two brothers. Their names are Ahmed and Ali. Which brother is the oldest? Explain your answer.

_____

_____

4 Put Nasreen and her brothers in age order. Explain your answer.

_____

_____

5 a Who are Nasreen's parents?

_____

b Explain how you know this.

_____

_____

_____

6 Predict the length of Meschack's father's upper arm bone. Explain your answer.

_____

_____

Exercise 1.4 Skeletons and movement

In this exercise, you will draw a diagram to explain how your muscles work.

Amira and Jessie made a model to show how muscles work. This is what their model looked like.

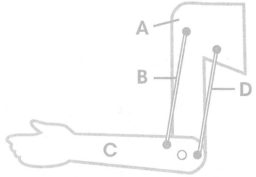

1 Write down the body parts for each of the labels A–D.

A _____

B _____

C _____

D _____

2 a What happens to part C when you pull up on part B?

_____

_____

b Make a drawing to show this.

3 Underline the correct words in the sentences to explain your drawing.

Part B relaxes/contracts and gets shorter/longer.

Part B pulls/pushes on part C and makes it drop/lift.

Exercise 1.5 Drugs as medicines

In this exercise, you will think about medicines.

1 Mark each of these statements as true [✔] or false [✘].

a   Drugs are substances that make your body
    change in some way. ☐

b   Medicines make us better when we are sick. ☐

c   Medicines are the same as drugs. ☐

d   Medicines cannot stop us from getting illnesses. ☐

2 Find **four** ways we take medicines in the word square.
Some words are written across the box and others are written
down the box.

i	n	j	e	c	t	i	o	n	t
n	w	e	r	t	y	n	i	o	a
h	a	s	d	f	g	h	n	l	b
a	c	b	i	u	n	l	t	h	l
l	e	d	b	n	t	m	m	d	e
e	v	f	p	o	w	d	e	r	t
r	u	r	k	l	g	o	n	i	u
m	i	x	t	u	r	e	t	p	m

3 Choose **three** different medicines. Complete the table to say
what each medicine is used for.

Medicine	What the medicine is used for

Exercise 1.6 How medicines work

In this exercise, you will identify unsafe ways of taking medicines.

1 Match each word to its meaning. The first one has been done for you.

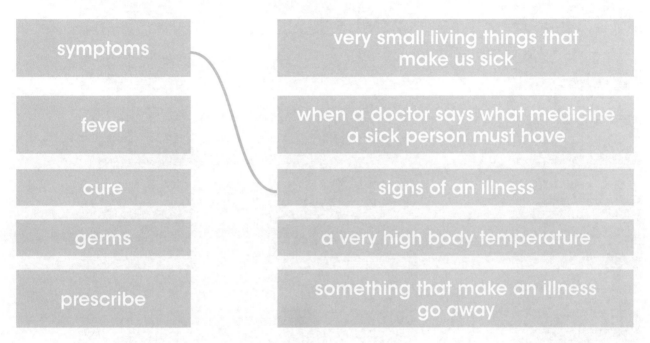

symptoms	very small living things that make us sick
fever	when a doctor says what medicine a sick person must have
cure	signs of an illness
germs	a very high body temperature
prescribe	something that make an illness go away

Yusef has a headache. He finds some tablets in the bathroom. He takes three tablets. Yusef has not taken this medicine safely.

2 Write down **four** things that are unsafe about the way he has taken this medicine.

> My mother takes these, so they must be okay.

_____

_____

_____

_____

Language review

1 This exercise checks that you understand the scientific words used in this unit. Match each word to its meaning. The first one has been done for you.

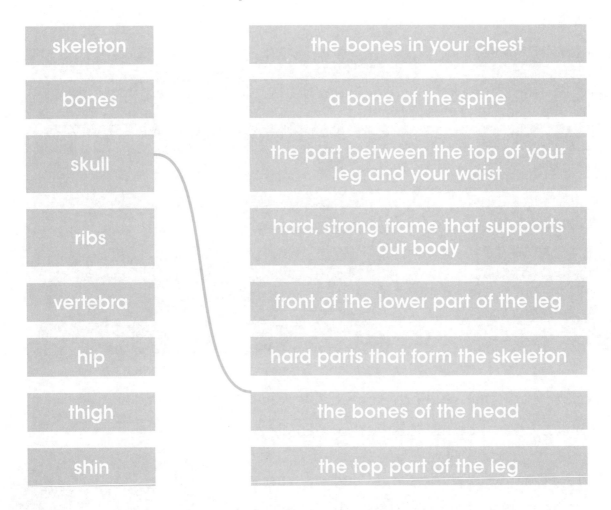

skeleton	the bones in your chest
bones	a bone of the spine
skull	the part between the top of your leg and your waist
ribs	hard, strong frame that supports our body
vertebra	front of the lower part of the leg
hip	hard parts that form the skeleton
thigh	the bones of the head
shin	the top part of the leg

2 Write one word for each of the underlined parts in these sentences.

When we are ill, we take <u>drugs that make our bodies better</u>. They can also <u>stop</u> us from getting ill. Sometimes we take these drugs as <u>dry substances made of very small grains</u>. If we are very ill in hospital, we may need <u>a piece of equipment that put medicines directly into our blood</u>.

2 Living things and environments

Exercise 2.1 Amazing birds

In this exercise, you will think about how birds' bodies help them in their environment.

Match the bird to the way its body helps it to live in its environment. The first one has been done for you.

webbed feet for swimming

lots of fat under the skin to keep body warm

long beak for getting nectar out of plants

long flat beak that allows it to shovel small fish from mud and water

skull shape allows eyes to see in front and below

Exercise 2.2 A habitat for snails

In this exercise, you will look at some information about snails that learners have collected.

Some learners were asked to count snails and note where they found them. Here are their results.

Place we looked	Number of snails found in 1 min
on the branch of a tree	0
under a stone	4
in a bush	2
under a log	10

1 Where were the most snails found?

_____

2 Why were many snails found here?

_____

_____

3 Where were the fewest snails found?

_____

4 Why was this?

_____

_____

In this exercise, you will look at a bar chart showing the numbers of dragonflies in a habitat.

Dragonflies need a habitat which includes a pond. They like warm weather and this is when they will breed.

A class of learners counted dragonflies every Wednesday for six weeks.

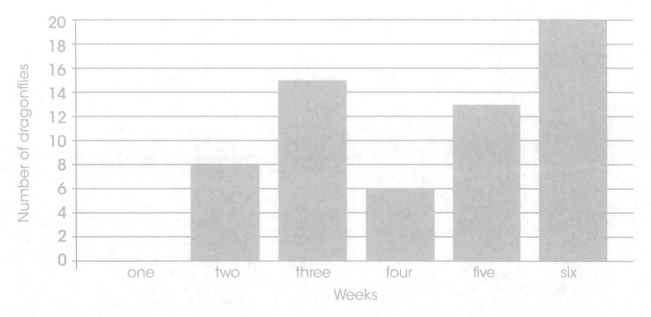

1 **What happened to the numbers of dragonflies over the six weeks?**

_____

2 **What do you think the weather was like in the first two weeks?**

_____

3 **Why might the numbers have changed in week four?**

_____

Exercise 2.4 Identification keys

In this exercise, you will complete a key about birds.

Place the birds shown here in the key.

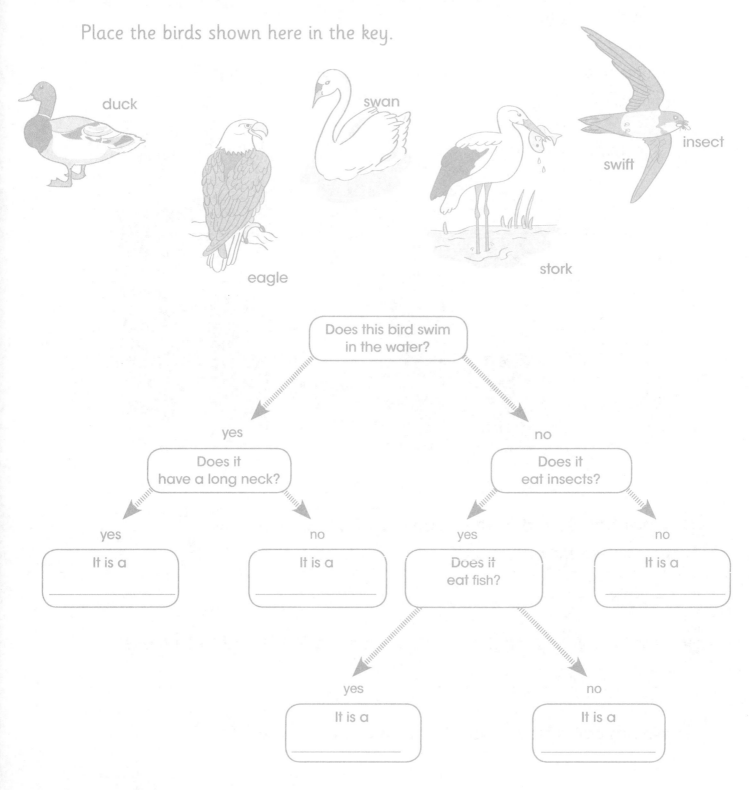

duck

swan

eagle

stork

swift

insect

Does this bird swim in the water?

yes

no

Does it have a long neck?

Does it eat insects?

yes

It is a
_____

no

It is a
_____

yes

Does it eat fish?

no

It is a
_____

yes

It is a
_____

no

It is a
_____

Identifying invertebrates

In this exercise, you complete a key for invertebrates.

dragonfly

butterfly

ladybird

bee

centipede

Look at the pictures of invertebrates.

Write the names of the invertebrates on the key.

worm

Does it have wings?

yes

no

Does it have one pair of wings?

Does it have many legs?

yes

no

yes

no

Does it have spots?

It is a
_____

It is a
_____

It is a
_____

yes

no

It is a
_____

Does it have patterned wings?

yes

no

It is a
_____

It is a
_____

In this exercise, you will think about things that we do to damage the environment.

Look at the picture. Circle the ways in which we have a bad effect on the environment.

Write down how we could reduce these bad effects.

_____

_____

_____

Exercise 2.7 Wonderful water

In this exercise, you will be thinking about animals that live in fresh water.

A class of learners studied a stream in their town. They observed animals at two different places along the stream.

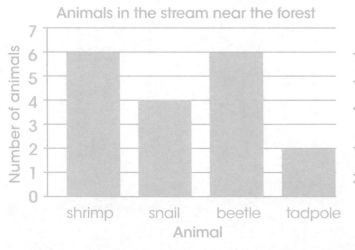

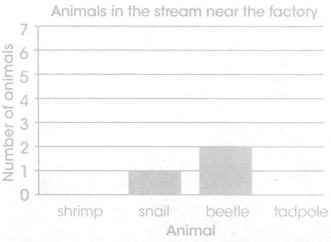

1 Where were most and fewest animals found?

_____

2 Which animal was the most common in the stream near the factory?

_____

3 Fish eat all these animals. Why were no fish found near the factory?

_____

4 What could be done to clean up the stream?

_____

_____

_____

In this exercise, you will think about recycling.

Sort these objects by drawing a line from each object to the correct bin.
The first one has been done for you.

DAILY NEWS

TV 7
NEW

1.5V4 'C'

9V PP9

♻ paper only

♻ plastic bottles only

♻ glass

♻ card

♻ cells

♻ food waste

Language review

This exercise checks that you understand the scientific words used in this unit.

1 Match each word to its meaning. The first one has been done for you.

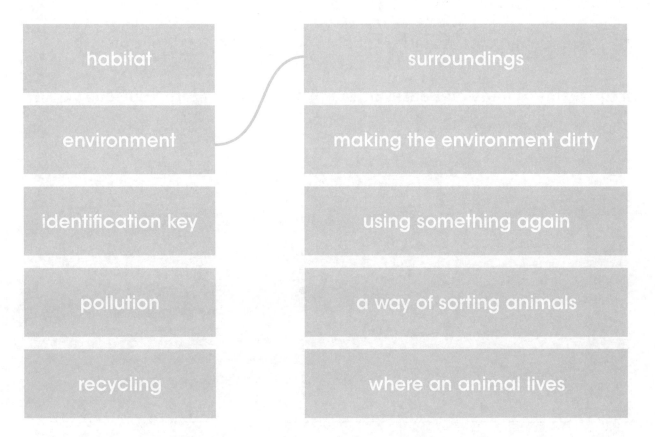

habitat	surroundings
environment	making the environment dirty
identification key	using something again
pollution	a way of sorting animals
recycling	where an animal lives

2 Fill in the gaps in these sentences. Use these words.

food   adapted   environment

Animals are _____ to help them to live in their habitats.

If an animal's _____ changes, it may change the way it behaves.

Animals need a habitat where there is _____ .

Solids, liquids and gases

3

Exercise 3.1 **Matter**

In this exercise, you will identify solids, liquids and gases from pictures.

Identify solids, liquids and gases in the pictures A–F. Write your answer in the space beside each picture.

A

B

C

_____

_____

_____

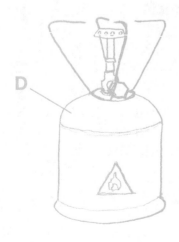

D

E

orange
juice

F

_____

_____

_____

In this exercise, you will make drawings to show how particles are arranged in solids, liquids and gases.

1 You have ten particles of matter. Draw the ten particles in each box below to represent a solid, a liquid and a gas.

solid	liquid	gas

2 Fill in the table to describe how particles move in the different states of matter.

State of matter	Do the particles move a lot, quite a lot or hardly at all?	Do the particles move apart, far apart or shake in one place?
solid		
liquid		
gas		

Exercise 3.3 How do solids, liquids and gases behave?

In this exercise, you will apply what you have learnt about the particle model of solids, liquids and gases to a new situation.

1 Look at the particles in the pictures of the two syringes, A and B.

a Which syringe contains water and which syringe contains air?

_____

b Use the particle model to explain your answer.

_____

_____

_____

_____

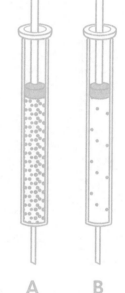

A   B

2 Look at the picture of the rain falling on the ground.

Draw an arrow on the picture to show where the water will be when the rain has stopped.

Exercise 3.4 Melting, freezing and boiling

In this exercise, you will identify melting, freezing and boiling in pictures.
Look at the pictures A–D below.

Write your answers to the questions in the table.

Picture	A	B	C	D
Name the type of matter (e.g. water).				
Identify the phase of the matter as it is now in the picture.				
Identify the phase change that has taken place to make this phase of matter (e.g. liquid to gas).				
Say whether the matter was heated or cooled to cause the phase change.				

Melting in different solids

In this exercise, you will use information in a table to answer questions about melting in different substances.

Substance	Melting point in °C
salt	800
sugar	185
ice	0
candle wax	60
chocolate	35

1 Describe the phase change that takes place when a substance melts.

_____

2 Which substance in the table melts at the highest temperature?

_____

3 Which substance in the table melts at the lowest temperature?

_____

4 Which substance needs the most heat to melt it?

_____

5 Room temperature is 22°C. Which substance will be liquid at room temperature?

_____

Exercise 3.6 Melting points

In this exercise, you will use information in a table to compare the melting points of different metals.

Metal	Melting point in °C
gold	1064
silver	962
aluminium	660
copper	1083

1 What is a melting point?

_____

2 List the metals in the order of highest melting point to the lowest melting point.

_____

_____

_____

_____

3 Complete the following phase change:

gold (_____ phase) $\xrightarrow[\text{_____ °C}]{\text{heat}}$ gold (_____ phase)

Language review

This exercise checks that you understand the scientific words used in this unit.

Write the correct words in the spaces within the sentences below using the following words. You will need to use some of these words more than once.

> temperature   particles   freezing point   liquid   gas   melt
> thermometer   freeze   solid   phase   matter   melting point

Everything consists of _____ . All matter consists of _____ . If the particles are closely packed so that they can only move a little bit, the substance is a _____ .

If the particles are more loosely packed so that they can slide over each other, the substance is a _____ .

If the particles are far apart and move a lot, the substance is a

_____ .

Heating causes a solid to _____ and change phase from solid to _____ . For example, when you heat a piece of butter, it changes from the _____ phase to the _____ phase.

Cooling causes a liquid to _____ . For example, water changes into ice. Freezing makes a substance change from the liquid _____ to the _____ phase.

We can measure the _____ at which a substance melts with a _____ . This is called the _____

_____ .

We can measure the _____ at which a substance freezes. This is called the _____ .

4 Sound

Exercise 4.1 Sound travels through materials

In this exercise, you will revise what you know about the materials that sound travels through.

1 Write the name of the sound source in each of these pictures.

A

B

C

D

a _____

b _____

c _____

d _____

2 Mark each of these statements as true [✔] or false [✗].

a Sound sometimes comes from a source. ☐

b You hear your friend whispering to you. This shows that sound travels through air. ☐

c When you hear your brother singing in the bathroom, it shows that sound travels through liquids. ☐

d When you hear rain on the roof, it shows that sound travels through solids. ☐

Sound travels through different materials

In this exercise, you will find information from a bar chart.

Liu and Ming listened to sounds through different materials. This is the bar chart they drew to show how loud the sounds were. Use the bar chart to answer the questions.

1 a   Is the material through which the sound was loudest a solid, liquid or gas?

_____

2 a   Liu and Ming also listened to sound through a wool hat. The loudness of the sound was 3 dB. Draw another bar on the bar chart to show this.

   b   Is wool a solid, liquid or gas?

_____

3 Which kinds of materials do sounds travel through best on the bar chart?

_____

Exercise 4.3 How sound travels

In this exercise, you will make a drawing to show the results of an investigation.

Look at the drawing.

1 Make a drawing to show what will happen if you tap gently on the jar with a pencil. Label all parts of the drawing.

2 Make a drawing to show what will happen if you tap hard on the jar with a pencil. Label all the parts of the drawing.

3 Use the words in the box to complete these sentences.

vibrations   more   less   vibrate

a   When you tap the jar it makes the rice grains _____ .

b   _____ travel through the jar and plastic wrap to the rice.

c   The rice grains move _____ when you tap the jar gently.

d   The rice grains move _____ when you tap the jar hard.

Exercise 4.4   Loud and soft sounds

In this exercise, you will remember what you
learnt about loudness.

You will apply what you know to a new situation.

1 Give an example of a loud sound.

_____

2 Give an example of a soft sound.

_____

3 How does the bell make a sound?

_____

4 Suggest as many ways you can think of to make the sound of
the bell ringing louder.

You can write sentences or draw pictures for your answer.

Exercise 4.5 Sound volume

In this exercise, you will match sounds with their loudness and compare the loudness of sounds. The first one has been done for you.

1 Draw a line from each of the sounds to match its loudness.

2 How loud do you think a Formula 1 racing car is? Is it softer, the same or louder than:

A   softer/same/louder

B   softer/same/louder

C   softer/same/louder

Exercise 4.6 Muffling sounds

In this exercise, you will
plan an investigation.

My sister's phone beeps all
the time when someone
leaves a message. How can I
make it quieter, Danji?

Maybe you should wrap
it up in a t-shirt, Amira.

1 a Which material did Danji suggest to
muffle the sound of the phone?

_____

b Write down **three** other materials that Amira and
Danji could test.

_____

_____

2 Write down **three** other pieces of equipment and apparatus that
they will need.

_____

_____

_____

3 What factor should they change and what **four** factors should
they keep the same?

_____

_____

Exercise 4.7   High and low sounds

In this exercise, you will apply what you know about changing the pitch of a stringed instrument.

Pedro has made a guitar. Look at the pictures of Pedro's guitar, A, B, C and D. So far he has only put in one string. Suppose Pedro presses on the string at point X and then plucks the string between X and Y.

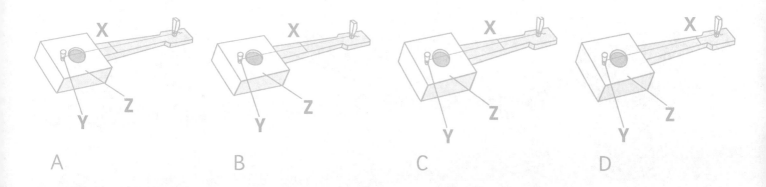

A   B   C   D

1 Will the pitch of sound be highest when the string is plucked between points X and Y in drawing A, B, C or D? Explain your answer.

_____

_____

2 How will the pitch of the sound change if the guitar string is thicker?

_____

_____

In this exercise, you will apply what you know about loud and soft sounds to percussion instruments.

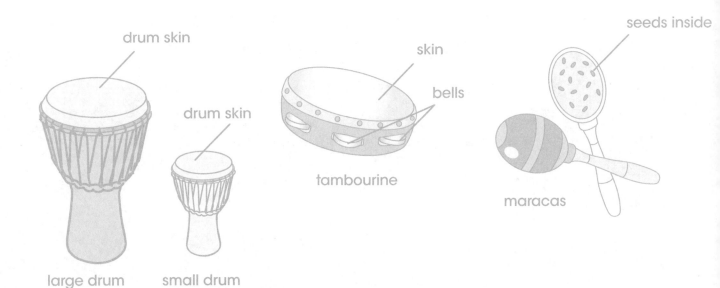

drum skin

drum skin

skin

bells

seeds inside

large drum   small drum

tambourine

maracas

1 Which instruments do you:

a   bang?

_____

b   shake?

_____

c   bang and shake?

_____

2 How do you make a louder sound with maracas?

_____

In this exercise, you will apply what you know about changing the pitch of a musical instrument.

1 What sort of musical instrument is this?

_____

2 How do you make a sound with this instrument?

_____

_____

_____

3 In which picture, A or B, is Huan making a higher pitched sound?

Write sentences to explain how you know. Use the words high pitch, low pitch, sound, vibrations, air-hole, column of air, shorter and longer, in your sentences.

_____

_____

_____

_____

Language review

This exercise checks that you understand the scientific words in this unit. Complete the words in the puzzle. Here are the clues for the words across.
Make up a clue for 1 down.

Clues across

1. _____ describes how high or low a sound is.

2. The unit for measuring the volume of sound is _____ .

3. We hear sounds when objects _____ .

4. Hitting a drum is a _____ of sound.

5. The opposite of a soft sound is a _____ sound.

6. Banjos and sitars are _____ instruments.

7. Leaves make a _____ sound when they move gently.

8. _____ instruments have pipes with air inside.

9. When you want the TV to be louder you turn up the _____ .

10. You can measure the volume of sound with a _____ level meter.

Clue down

1. _____

5 Electricity and magnetism

Exercise 5.1 Electricity flows in circuits

In this exercise, you will apply what you know about electric current flowing around a circuit.

Rafaela's baby brother has a cell-operated toy car. The toy needs two cells to make it work.

Rafaela puts two cells into the car, but it doesn't work. Rafaela's brother starts to cry.

Then Rafaela takes the cells out, turns one of the cells around and puts them back in the car. This time the car goes. Rafaela's brother is happy!

1 **Why didn't the car go when Rafaela put the cells in the first time?**

_____

_____

2 **Why did the car go when Rafaela changed the cells?**

_____

cell   motor

_____

3 **Here is a drawing of the inside of the toy car.**

a   Mark the positive and negative ends of the cells.

b   Draw arrows to show the path of the electrical current.

Exercise 5.2 Components and a simple circuit

In this exercise, you will apply what you know about components and what they do in a circuit.

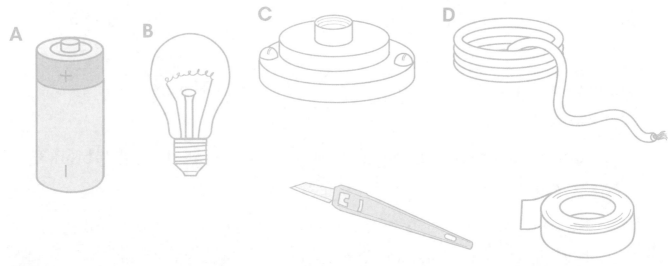

A   B   C   D

1 Complete this sentence.

A, B, C and D are electrical _____ .

2 What does the cell provide?

_____

3 Why do you need a bulb holder?

_____

_____

4 Why must the plastic from the ends of the wire be cut off?

_____

_____

_____

Exercise 5.3 Switches

In this exercise, you will apply what you know about switches.

1 What does a switch do in a circuit?

_____

_____

2 Look at this picture.

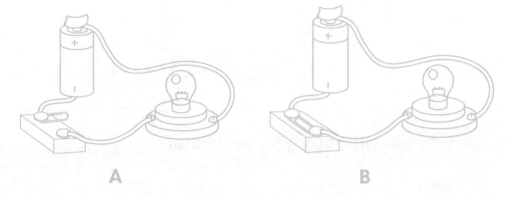

A   B

In which of the two circuits, A or B, will the bulb light up?
Explain your answer.

_____

_____

_____

3 What do we mean by 'a break in the circuit'?

_____

_____

_____

Exercise 5.4 Circuits with more components

In this exercise, you will apply what you know about circuits with different numbers of cells and bulbs.

Look at this circuit.

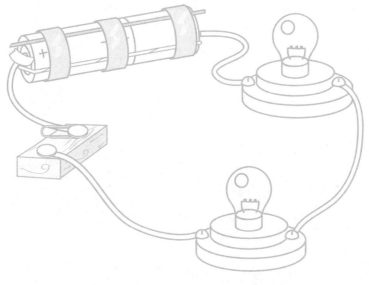

1 Write down **five** components in the circuit.

_____

_____

2 What must you do to the circuit before the bulbs will light up?

_____

_____

3 You add another bulb to this circuit. What happens to the bulbs? **Explain your answer.**

_____

_____

Exercise 5.5 Circuits with buzzers

In this exercise, you will apply what you know about circuits and voltage of components.

Rosalie and Eugenie made a circuit with a 3V buzzer. They had to change their circuit several times before the buzzer worked.

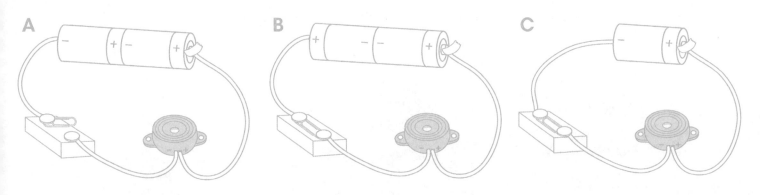

1 Explain why the buzzer did not work properly in circuit A.

_____

_____

2 Explain why the buzzer did not work properly in circuit B.

_____

_____

3 Explain why the buzzer did not work properly in circuit C.

_____

_____

Exercise 5.6 Mains electricity

In this exercise, you will apply what you know about using mains electricity safely.

For each picture, is electricity used safely or dangerously?

Write a sentence to explain your answer in each case.

A _____

_____

B _____

_____

C _____

_____

Exercise 5.7 Magnets in everyday life

In this exercise, you will apply what you know about magnets.

Write the correct words in the spaces. Choose your words from this list.

> closed   magnetism   steel   magnetic   bar   keepers   wand

A magnet can attract certain objects to it. Examples are **pins** and **nails.**

A magnet can attract certain materials to it. An example is

_____. Materials that are attracted by a magnet are

called _____ materials.

A fridge door has strip magnets down the side of the door. These magnets

help to keep the door _____ firmly.

Three types of magnets are horseshoe, _____ and _____ magnets.

All magnets lose their _____ if you drop them or bang them

together. You must store magnets with _____ on their

ends to keep them strong.

Exercise 5.8 Magnetic poles

In this exercise, you will apply what you know about poles of magnets.

1 Fill in the spaces in these sentences.

a A magnet has a north pole and a _____ pole.

b Like poles _____ one another.

c Unlike poles _____ one another.

2 For each pair of magnets, draw arrows to show which way the magnets will move. The first one has been done for you.

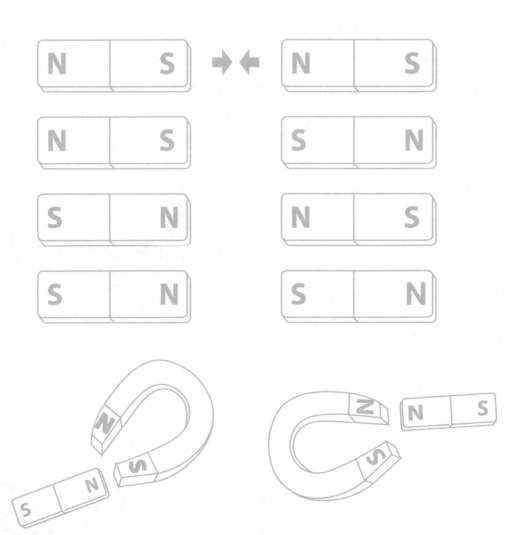

Exercise 5.9 Strength of magnets

In this exercise, you will apply what you know about measuring the strength of a magnet.

Lorenzo compares the strength of two bar magnets, A and B. He has three pieces of card 10 × 10 cm and a steel screw.

This is what Lorenzo does.

He places the screw on a table underneath one piece of card. He holds magnet A over the card. The screw sticks to the card and he is able pick up the card and screw with the magnet.

He repeats this with magnet B and gets the same result.

He now puts two pieces of card between the magnet and the screw. The screw still sticks to the card when he uses magnet A and magnet B.

He now puts three pieces of card between the magnet and the screw. The screw still sticks to the card when he uses magnet A. But when he uses magnet B the screw does not stick to the card.

1 Why does the screw stick to the card when Lorenzo holds a magnet over the card?

_____

_____

2 Which magnet was strongest, A or B? Explain why.

_____

_____

3 In what ways was Lorenzo's experiment a fair test?

_____

_____

4 Could Lorenzo have used a cork or a plastic button instead of a screw to test the strength of the magnets? Explain your answer.

_____

_____

Which metals are magnetic?

In this exercise, you will apply what you know about magnetic and non-magnetic metals.

brass window catch

steel kettle

copper wire

aluminium foil dish

stainless steel knives

stainless steel draining board

iron pot scourer

stainless steel forks

cast iron cooking pot

Decide whether each metal shown in the picture is magnetic or non-magnetic.

Fill in your answers on this table.

Object	Magnetic	Non-magnetic

Language review

This exercise checks that you understand the scientific words used in this unit. Look at the balloons below. Each balloon contains a key word from this unit. The letters are scrambled.

Unscramble the letters in balloons 1–12. Write the word in the space by each balloon.

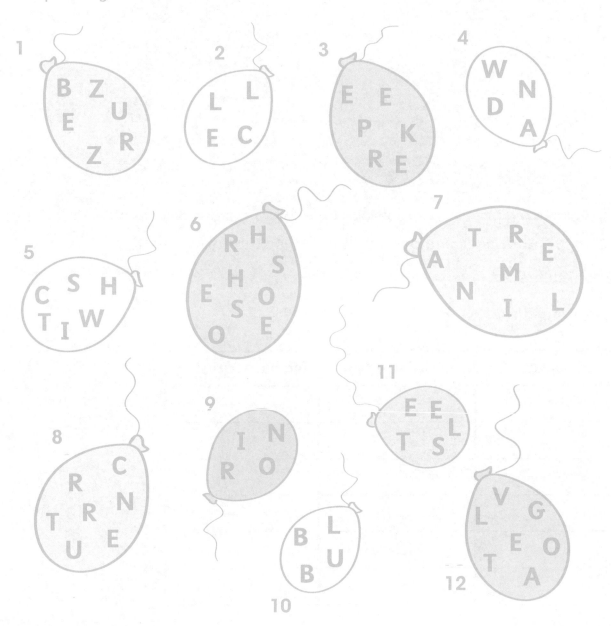

1 B Z U R E Z E

2 L L E C

3 E E P K R E

4 W N D A

5 C S H T I W

6 R H S H S E O S O E

7 A T R E R M I N L

8 R C R T R N E U E

9 I N R O

10 B L U B

11 E E T L S

12 L V G L E O T A